7 Days To Confident Interviews

Ericka Spradley

7 Days To Confident Interviews

Meet Ericka Spradley, Career Coach

Meet "the planner who didn't have a plan." Ericka spent 18 years of her life "stuck" in a vicious cycle beginning with her first job at the age of 16. As a matter of fact, she wasn't sure of her strengths and couldn't identify her "dream job" for most of her professional career. In spite of that, Ericka managed to successfully interview and secure employment with the following employers:

- Office Warehouse
- Sports Authority
- Upton's
- Bed, Bath & Beyond
- GAP
- Bose Corporation
- The Disney Store
- Talbot's
- Wachovia Bank
- Wells Fargo

In January 2006, Ericka took a leap of faith that changed everything! She wanted to attend Sunday church services and retail management demands would not allow her to do so. She did the unthinkable: she withdrew the balance in her 401k, left her employer after providing a 6-week notice, uploaded her resume to Monster.com and went on vacation! While on vacation, she received a call from a recruiter in the banking industry. In speaking with the recruiter, Ericka was told she qualified for 2 positions that were available. She decided to take the route of Financial Center Manager. The very next month,

Ericka transitioned into banking without any experience and without a college degree. She learned a valuable lesson during that time: skills are transferrable. From the initial employment opportunity at the age of 16 and throughout her career, Ericka's ability to interview served as a lifeline; the skill she needed to succeed when she didn't have a college degree.

Ericka relocated the following year, continued to pursue her education and discovered her passion while attending Strayer University: interviewing. Out of this discovery, My Next Level was birthed in 2010 but her path to success has been anything but traditional. She truly understands the connection between the successful interview, employment, compensation and having your basic needs met. She describes her love for coaching others to interview successfully as "oxygen" and was born to equip, empower and encourage others with the gift she has been given. Her ability to demonstrate necessary skills for a position through communication have served her well. Ericka plans to spend the rest of her life equipping others with effective interviewing skills so they, too can successfully secure employment.

Overview

Welcome to 7 Days to Confident Interviews!! You've decided, or someone has decided for you that your professional future is important. In understanding this simple fact, you're well on your way to improving a pivotal skill needed for achieving goals along your career path. The reality is simple: when you interview successfully, you stand a better chance of receiving a job offer. 7 Days to Confident Interviews is a practical approach to interview preparation designed to increase your confidence as well as your level of preparedness. However, you must be willing to follow the steps as outlined in this book and do the work ahead of time. The secret to successful interviews is in your ability to communicate your skills effectively and in your level of dedication to preparedness.

This book:

- Equips, empowers and encourages you to take appropriate steps that lead to securing employment via effective interview preparation
- Provides daily next steps to improve preparedness
- Allows you to self-assess and identify skills and experiences that align with the position you seek *before* the interview

- Assists with preparation to decrease "silent" moments *during* the interview; which tends to diminish confidence

This book is for you if:

- Interviewing makes you nervous
- You're unfamiliar with behavioral-based interviews
- You "draw a blank" during interviews
- You're uncertain about your ability to interview successfully
- You're contacted for interviews but aren't receiving job offers

I applaud you for dedicating the next 7 days to equipping yourself for interview success. Please read the material in its entirety; in the order presented and be sure to complete the daily activities "Your next steps" for best results. Let's get started!!

Day 1: Introduction to Interviews

What is the purpose of an interview? This is the most important phase of the job search that involves a conversation between a job applicant and a representative of the employing organization. It provides a candidate with the opportunity to showcase skills and experience necessary for the role in addition to asking questions of the potential employer. During the interview, both the candidate and hiring personnel have an opportunity to pose questions to determine fit, but the employer's purpose is to select the best employee.

What is behavioral-based interviewing? It is designed to determine whether or not an applicant has the necessary skill set for a position. The belief with this style of interviewing is that past behavior indicates future performance. Therefore, your responses should "tell a brief, concise story" demonstrating exceptional use of the skills necessary for success in the role, which we will review in the days ahead.

What will it take to succeed during a behavioral interview? You must first identify the skills needed for the role. Once you've identified skills and practice questions, you can then begin to prepare your responses. It will take preparation and practice of your responses prior to an interview to increase your chances of success. Note: To locate practice questions, enter the following in your search engine of choice:

"skill" behavioral-based interview questions. For example, if you've identified customer service as a skill needed for the role, enter "customer service behavioral-based interview questions" in the search engine. Your search results will produce information containing practice questions for each skill you enter.

Key Interview Components Showcasing YOU!!

- Cover Letter: A document addressed to your employer that accompanies your resume. Your cover letter explains suitability for the role and provides additional information detailing your skills/experience. Note: your cover letter should not exceed 1 page.

- Resume: A written compilation of your education, work experience, credentials, and accomplishments used to apply for jobs. When leveraged properly, your resume can open the door to the interview. Note: Because there are various resume types, decide whether a chronological, functional or combination resume will work best for you.

- Interview: A process in which a potential employee is evaluated by an employer for prospective employment in their organization. During this process, the employer hopes to determine whether or not the applicant is suitable for the role. Candidates who interview successfully have a greater chance of receiving employment offers.

Your next steps: Define the purpose of an interview and behavioral interviewing. Next, prepare responses to the following to cultivate self-awareness prior to an interview:

- Describe your dream job; specific location (city and state), name or title of desired position and annual salary.

- What are your workplace strengths? List 3-5.

- What are your career goals? Is there are a particular field of interest, organization or position you're interested in?

- What are your areas of opportunity i.e. weaknesses? List 1-2.

- List the top 5 skills you possess.

Day 2: Interviewing is Mental

Your mindset during the interview process can work for you or against you. The good news is that it doesn't take any more energy to practice optimism than it does negativity. It comes down to a decision, which you are capable of controlling. If you've said and/or thought the following, your mindset is working against you.

- "I absolutely hate to interview."
- "Interviews make me nervous."
- "I'm horrible at interviewing."

I once read when you change your thinking; you can change your life. This requires removing barriers and self-imposed limits to access the creativity necessary for goal achievement. In other words, you have to replace the negative thoughts and words with positive words and behaviors to achieve your desired outcome.

Your next steps: Make a list of self-limiting beliefs pertaining to the interview such as "Interviewing makes me nervous" or "I'm terrible at interviewing" and replace them with positive, affirming statements. Read your statements aloud 3 times per day to reinforce a positive belief system instead of a negative one. Then prepare your responses to the following:

- What do you feel is limiting you?

- What will it take for you to believe you can interview successfully? Hint: Everything starts with a decision followed by behaviors to achieve the desired outcome.

Day 3: Interview Support System

I was contacted by a client who rescheduled her interview due to a panic attack. I assist from time to time as she attempts to secure employment, which means I'm an integral part of her support system. Although you may not experience this type of anxiety, it doesn't mean you don't require support as you seek employment opportunities. I highly recommend identifying persons who can assist you with mock interviews and/or offer support. Benefits of having a support system when you prepare for an interview include:

- Positive outlook and emotional support
- Additional information and resources
- Enhanced effectiveness of responses
- Improvement in interpersonal communication

Your next steps: Respond to the following and then implement a plan that includes people who will help you achieve professional success.

- In terms of your professional success, who is hindering you?

- Who will assist you with the interviewing process and help you achieve your professional goals?

- List the names of those in your ideal support system. Evaluate who you currently have for support and who you'd like to have support you. Make the necessary changes within your support system as soon as possible.

Day 4: Interview Tips

Employment candidates will need effective interviewing skills if the goal is to remain competitive and ultimately secure employment. Today we'll review interview do's and don'ts, common interview mistakes and virtual interview tips.

Interview Do's:

- Dress professionally
- Arrive early (early is the equivalent of on time in the business world)
- Silence your phone
- Communicate professionally and effectively verbally and in writing
- Prepare ahead of time by practicing responses to interview questions
- Sell yourself by speaking to your skill set, experience and qualifications for the role
- Ask questions pertaining to the role and organization
- Follow-up with a thank you note

Interview Don'ts:

- Don't monitor the time by watching a clock, checking your phone or glancing at your watch
- Don't assume you know the question being asked; listen
- Don't be afraid to pause a few seconds before answering

- Don't exaggerate your accomplishments
- Don't chew gum
- Don't exhibit frustrations or a negative attitude
- Don't go to extremes with your posture; don't slouch or sit rigidly on the edge of your chair
- Don't make negative comments about others, previous employers, etc.

Virtual Interview Tips

- Prepare as if the interview is face-to-face. Although the number of phone and virtual interviews are increasing, it's still in your best interest to communicate thoughtful, organized, appropriate responses to questions that will demonstrate the skills needed for success in the role.

- Be professional in appearance and familiarize yourself with the technology you're using, i.e. audio and visual technology. If possible, have an "interview rehearsal" to ensure your image sounds and looks appropriate for your interview.

- Minimize/eliminate background noise. I would suggest a quiet place minus interruptions and distractions. Background noise may cause an interviewer to miss pertinent information you're attempting to convey, which could negatively impact you.

- Use a landline telephone if possible. Although mobile devices are the new norm, dropped calls are a reality. Not only will you have to speak clearly and slowly, you want to avoid the possibility of having interference during the interview.

Common interview mistakes:

- Neglecting to use "I". The objective isn't arrogance; it's confidence in your ability to demonstrate your fit for the role and organization. When you arrive for an interview; you must show up to articulate your skills. Please avoid using a collection of examples that demonstrate what he, she and they did unless you're providing a response that demonstrates a specific skill, i.e. teamwork or building strategic partnerships. Be comfortable with sharing *your* experiences and how they can positively impact the organization.

- Failing to practice. Some candidates have a natural fear of speaking in front of others and the way to overcome that fear is to practice. Share a copy of the job description with someone who will provide helpful feedback. Read your examples to them; then ask for their opinions and suggestions, which should ultimately improve the quality of your responses.

- Using vague examples. Find a delicate balance between sharing enough detail in a concise manner and not rambling on. Please understand that whoever is conducting the interview must have enough detail from the examples you provide to determine whether or not you have the skills/experience needed to perform in the role. More often than not, interviewers don't have a lot of "extra" time, so communicate effectively while you have the opportunity.

- Eliminating negative thoughts. One of the worst things you can do prior to an interview is remind yourself how terrible you are at interviewing, how much confidence you lack and how you hate to interview. You will probably achieve what you believe, so remain positive. Encourage yourself, practice and above all else, give your best!

- Showing up empty handed. By providing the interviewer with a copy of your portfolio (7-8 pages max.) which should include your: cover letter, resume, letters of recommendation, awards/recognition, etc. you're demonstrating professionalism, preparedness and organizational skills which can certainly benefit an employer.

- Asking the recruiter to tell you about the organization. It's your responsibility to arrive prepared and knowledgeable about the company. In addition, please avoid inquiries pertaining to salary, paid time away, etc. during the first (and in some cases second) round of interviews. These discussions are more appropriate once you're aware that an offer will be extended.

- Using examples that make you seem unfavorable. Although time management might be your area of opportunity, demonstrate how you've turned it into a strength that is currently being improved or has been improved. Too many "areas of opportunity" can decrease your chance of being viewed as the best candidate for the role, which decreases your chances of securing employment.

- Getting too comfortable. Don't relax to the point where you become unprofessional. Always use proper etiquette, appropriate grammar, and arrive early; professionally dressed. Professionalism is the standard and shouldn't be considered optional during your interview.

- Neglecting to silence your cell phone. If you decide not to power off your device, you can turn your ringer off as an alternative. Unnecessary cell phone interruptions during an interview will diminish your level of professionalism.

  Additional tips can be found via the "Interview Mistakes" tab at: www.ErickaSpradley.com.

Your next steps: Avoid the common interview mistakes listed in this book as well as the additional tips found on my website.

Day 5: Pre-Interview Questions

Pre-interview (background) questions are typically asked prior to behavioral questions during an interview and are sometimes posed during the phone screening process. *[Phone screen: allows the employer to determine if a candidate's qualifications, experience, salary and preferences align with the role.]* Today, we'll examine background questions and what to consider when responding to them.

What is the purpose of pre-interview (background) questions? These questions allow employers to gather pertinent information about you aside from your resume, cover letter and letters of recommendation.

Why ask pre-interview (background) questions? The objective is to ask questions that aren't posed during the "actual interview"; to find out if you're a fit for both the role and the organization. You can typically respond to these questions in 2-3 sentences.

Please keep in mind that your responses to behavioral interview questions will be longer than your responses to background questions. You know the question is behavioral when it begins with:

- "Describe how you handled…."
- "Tell me about a situation in which you…."
- "Give me an example of a time when…."

Whether it's a background question or a behavioral question, remember to pause and think through your answer before speaking. Knowing where your response ends before you begin to speak conveys clarity of thought, organization of speech and confidence.

Examples of Pre-Interview (Background) Questions

- Tell me about yourself.
- Why are you interested in this position?
- What do you like the most/least about your current job?
- Why are you the best candidate for this role?
- Where do you see yourself in the next __ years?

When these background questions are presented, use the tips below to formulate your responses.

Tell me about yourself.

Mention information pertinent to work experience, i.e. skills and qualifications. In other words, show the correlation between your previous or existing experience and the role you're applying for.

Why are you interested in this position?

Talk about the organization, trends in the industry and why the role is a fit for you as a candidate. Consider the value you bring to the organization.

Include information that encompasses more than the role you're applying for. For example, you're interviewing for a Project Manager role, but you have experience in other areas that will possibly benefit the organization. You could say: *"Although my experience is in project management, I also have an extensive background in customer service which allowed me to build relationships, retain clients and increase revenues through sales. According to your website, the company has locations in international markets. Long term, I would love to secure a role where I can use my ability to manage projects effectively along with my sales and customer service background to build strategic partnerships internationally."*

What do you like the most/least about your current job?

- Be honest but present the negative as a positive.
- Discuss strengths and how you deal with those challenges.
- Don't like your role? Instead of expressing discontent, try: *"The environment is unorganized*

and there is limited room for advancement. However, I recognize there is an opportunity to help with organization and structure within the department, so I've scheduled a meeting with my leader to see how I can assist."

Why are you the best candidate for this role?

- Set yourself apart from the competition.
- Be confident without being arrogant.
- Re-emphasize your experience and qualifications. They should directly reflect the skills and qualifications that are outlined in the job description.

Where do you see yourself in the next __ years?

- Know what your plans are for your career both short-term and long-term so you can articulate your vision/strategy.

Additional examples of background questions:

- How do you stay abreast of trends in your field?
- What have you done in the last year to continue your learning/education?
- What is your motivation to succeed?

- Besides qualifications and experience, why do you feel we should choose you over other aspiring candidates?
- What do you know about this organization/position?
- What prompted you to apply with our company?
- What are some of the things you value in an employer?
- If you had only one word to describe yourself, what would it be? Why?
- What challenges do you foresee in this type of job and how would you overcome them?

Your next steps: Practice and prepare responses to the background questions listed in Day 5 of this book.

Day 6: Effective Responses

Responses can be effective or ineffective during an interview. Unfortunately, some employment hopefuls can't discern one from the other. Remember: content is king, not necessarily the length of your response. Ultimately you want to "speak the language of skills" through your responses. In order to do this, you must: (1) identify the skills necessary for the role (2) capture your BEST examples demonstrating skill proficiency (3) communicate those responses professionally and with confidence during the interview.

What does an effective response include? A beginning, a middle and an ending. If you think of your responses as a story, every great story has a beginning, a middle and an ending. The content of your response ("your story") must be confident, organized, easy to follow and communicated effectively, so:
- State the specific situation (the beginning)
- Explain the steps to resolution in detail (the middle)
- Share the outcome of the steps you've taken (the ending)

Effective response tips:

- Prepare detailed examples. Employers want specifics - not generalizations.
- The situation as well as the result shouldn't exceed 2-3 sentences.
- The detailed steps you took to achieve the outcome is the lengthiest part of your response

(the middle of "your story"). This is how the employer assesses skill set for the question posed.

- Quantify your answers; use numbers when you share your achievements/results.
- Give specific information in your answer such as department names, length of time to resolve an issue, etc.
- Pause and think through your answer before starting; know where your story ends before you begin to speak.
- You **must** have a complete response. The interviewer(s) cannot assess your skill set when incomplete responses are provided.
- Avoid acronyms such as SLA (Service Level Agreement) to avoid confusion. The interviewer may not be familiar with organizational jargon.

Please read the responses below and respond with "true" or "false".

The following is an effective response to a behavioral interview question.

"In the past, I have demonstrated my ability to go above and beyond to enhance a project. I have worked extra hours, negotiated for additional resources on my projects, and utilized technology to save time and money. I always strive for the best possible result, even if it meant extra work on my part. I feel it's worth it to kick in the additional effort in order to have a project outcome that will benefit the company. You'll find that I'm constantly looking for ways to get the best result possible."

True or false: The following is an effective response to a behavioral interview question.

"In situations such as these, I would consider the extra effort I'd need to input in relationship to output. I would also consider the value for the project. If the value was great enough, I would work extra hours in order to improve the project. Ultimately, I know the project would have a better outcome and my team would be recognized for the exceptional work."

If you answered false for both examples, you are correct! If you can't identify a specific situation, the steps taken **AND** an outcome, then the response is ineffective in a behavioral- based interview. Please keep this in mind as you prepare and practice your responses.

*Example of an effective response: "Tell me about a time a problem you solved."

We were receiving complaints about late deliveries. **(State the situation; the beginning)**

I scheduled a meeting and met with the 10 associates involved in the customer delivery department. I discovered the problem; stock wasn't coming through on time based on feedback from the department. I researched and found that requests for new inventory were not being processed efficiently. The backlog was in the orders department as they were not following up adequately with the suppliers. I implemented a system for consistent follow up, thus holding the team accountable and rewarding them for a job well done. **(Explain the steps taken: the middle)**

My implemented system resolved our stock problems and the delivery staff was able to meet their deadlines, thus eliminating our complaints about late deliveries. Customer complaints were reduced by 75% within 3 weeks based on the system I created. **(The outcome; the ending)**

*Example of an effective response: "Tell me about a time when you were under extreme pressure to meet a deadline."

One of my current responsibilities is to act as a liaison between departments to ensure our ad-hoc mailings are released into the mail stream by the project deadline. In this particular instance, I was notified of a rush mailing, with a volume of 19,000 letters and senior leaders were requesting the outcome of this mailing. **(State the situation; the beginning)**

On average, I have 2-3 days upon receiving files to perform the steps necessary to meet the deadline for a mailing. Those steps include: requesting print samples, scanning samples into a PDF and sending them to an internal client for approval via email. Upon receiving approval, I then partner with our print and rendering teams via email to process the mailing. Once the mailing is printed and rendered, I perform a quality control measure and capture the data in a spreadsheet, which I then send to our internal client. When I receive approval of the quality control measure, I release the mailing. With this particular rush mailing, I received the files after 5pm on the day the mailing was due to be released into the mail stream. I shared with my leader that I would stay late to ensure this mailing went through the proper process as I mentioned, from samples sent to the quality control measure. I performed each of these steps with our rush mailing as I do with all of our ad-hoc mailings, but in a reduced amount of time; in a matter of hours vs. 2-3 days. Throughout this process, I constantly communicated with leadership and internal partners to ensure flawless execution of the project. (Explain the actions taken; the middle)

As a result, the mailing was processed and released before 9:00pm, which means we met the deadline for our rush mailing. The next day, I was recognized by one of our partners for my dedication as well as my ability to deliver exceptional service. (The outcome; the ending)

Note: This is the time to really think about the skills you possess; those the employer desires in their ideal candidate. When you share your responses, you are "speaking the language of skills". In essence, you're sharing favorable responses that completely answer the question posed, thus demonstrating skill proficiency. As you evaluate the sample interview questions used for practice in this book, notice the behavioral-based questions are asking about a specific skill. Your effective response should demonstrate the skill the employer is asking about.

Potential questions to ask during an interview:
During an interview you should always ask questions, specifically ones that offer information; ones that can't be found on the company's website or in the job posting. You will want to obtain as much information as possible to ensure the position is a fit for you. Here are actual questions I've posed in the past as well as the reasons why:

*What are some of the challenges in this line of business and in the organization? Every company has challenges and it's important for you to understand that this information isn't typically shared in an interview. You are selling yourself as the best person for the job and the organization is being sold during this process as well. You certainly want to know the strengths and weaknesses of the department and organization prior to accepting a role.

*Describe your current work environment in one word. Once this question is answered, probe to find out why this particular description was used. The response will provide insight in terms of the climate within the department.

*What has the organization done to attract and retain the best talent? I've never worked for an organization that didn't want the best and brightest talent. If the hiring manager can't tell you what's being done to develop and retain the existing talent within the organization, what will happen to your development should you accept an offer?

*Aside from the information outlined for this position, can you describe the ideal candidate for this role? Typically, the hiring manager has an idea of what type of person would be perfect for the open position. If the hiring manager is interested in a strong team player, your passion in an interview regarding teamwork could potentially determine whether or not you will receive an offer. If given the opportunity to share anything else after you ask questions, you can speak to your strengths that parallel the ones mentioned for the ideal candidate.

Your next steps: Select 5 questions and prepare your responses to ensure they contain the components of an effective response.

- Please give your best example of working cooperatively with someone who didn't share the same ideas.

- Tell me about a time when you took the initiative to learn more about a product/service.

- Give an example of a time in which you had to be relatively quick in coming to a decision.

- Tell us about a difficult experience you had in working with details.

- Tell us about a problem you solved in a unique or unusual way.

- Describe a time when you were asked to keep information confidential.

- Give an example of a time when you made a mistake because you didn't listen to what was said.

- Describe a situation where you were able to use persuasion to successfully convince someone to see things your way.

- Describe a situation that required you to do a number of things at the same time.

- Tell us about a time when you made an intentional effort to get to know someone from another culture.

As you prepare your responses, feel free to organize each response in this way:

- Beginning (specific situation)
- Middle (detailed action steps)
- Ending (the outcome of the situation)

Doing so allows you to assess whether or not your response is complete and you can perform edits as you see fit.

Day 7: Practice, Practice, Practice!

Benefits of practice:

- Increases confidence
- Organization of thought
- Identification of skills and experiences needed for the role
- Effective communication during the interview
- Ability to obtain feedback *before* the interview
- Decreases instances where you "draw a blank" during the interview

Your next steps: According to a NACE Job Outlook Survey, the list below includes attributes/skills employers seek. In addition, I've provided practice interview questions so you can edit your responses to sheer perfection. Please ensure your response contains a beginning, a middle and an ending. Feel free to visit information from Day 6 to ensure your responses are effective.

- Leadership/initiative: Tell us about a time when you led a team.
- Problem-solving skills: Tell us about a problem you solved.
- Written/verbal communication skills: Describe a time when you had to build a successful relationship.
- Teamwork: Describe your most recent group effort.

- Technical/computer skills: Tell me about a recent assignment you had involving technology.
- Strong work ethic: Describe your work ethic.
- Analytical skills: Give an example of a time when you had to analyze information that was unfamiliar.

Additional Practice Questions:

- Tell us about a time you had to adapt to a difficult situation.

- Describe the most complex project you've managed from start to finish.

- Tell me about a time when you managed a diverse team.

- Give an example of how you react when faced with constant pressure.

- Tell me about a time when you had an angry customer.

- Tell me about an assignment you worked on in which you had to amass a huge amount of data and then analyze it.

- Please give me a specific example of how you obtained information to solve a problem.

- Give an example of a time when your work group or department worked with another work group or department to accomplish a goal, but encountered challenges during the process.

- Tell me about a time when you led a project that your team wasn't enthusiastic about.

- Tell me about a time when you had to cultivate and maintain a relationship.

- Tell me about a time when you implemented and coordinated a team effort in which you served as a liaison for the group and a subject matter expert.

- Tell us about a time when you had to communicate complex information.

- Describe a situation when you had to exercise a significant amount of self-control.

- Tell me about a time when you had to help someone settle a dispute.

- Give an example of time when you've built motivation in others.

- Tell me about a time when you were responsible for a budget and you overspent allocated funds.

10 Commandments of Interviewing

1. Thou shalt develop a next level mindset.
2. Thou shalt keep the faith and not doubt.
3. Thou shalt apply knowledge obtained from a professional and eliminate guesswork.
4. Thou shalt breath, live and exude confidence.
5. Thou shalt master the art of behavioral-based interviews.
6. Thou shalt evaluate thy circle, eliminating negativity and non-supportive interactions.
7. Thou shalt prepare after you apply for jobs; acting as if you've been contacted for the interview.
8. Thou shalt incorporate consistency, focus and discipline.
9. Thou shalt dedicate a minimum of 5 hours to preparation and practice of responses.
10. Thou shalt not experience interview regret.

Article: Taking Your Interview to the Next Level

As a professional, performing in the role is simply what we do. We are the dream chasers, the subject matter experts and the mentor of many mentees. Yet amidst these wonderful things, we often sell ourselves short during employment interviews. The reason for this is simple: there is a different language used in interviews that we typically don't use day to day. The question isn't about qualifications nor is it about an exceptional resume that can open the door to an interview. The question is: "Will you be able to convince the interviewer you're the best person for the role based on your responses?" If the answer isn't an unequivocal YES, this article will serve as a catalyst to improve your ability to interview successfully. Below you'll find 3 tips that will certainly take your interview to the next level:

1. Be mindful of what you think: interviewing is mental. Your mindset during the interview can work for you or against you. The good news is that it doesn't take any more energy to practice optimism than it does negativity. It comes down to a decision, which you are capable of controlling. I once read when you change your thinking; you can change your life. This requires removing barriers and self-imposed limits to access the creativity necessary for goal achievement (see Day 2). In essence, you have to replace the negative thoughts and words with positive words and behaviors to achieve your desired outcome, which is interview success.

2.   Be mindful of what you do: PRACTICE! In my mind, the interview is the championship game. In other words, not only do I have to prepare before the "big game", I have to practice my responses long before the game begins. Unfortunately, candidates are now waiting to prepare once they are contacted for an interview; that's too late to prepare due to time constraints and it's costing them the job. Not only is preparation and practice ongoing, you want to prepare exemplary examples based on your qualifications. Remember: content is king, not necessarily the length of your response. If you think of your responses as a story, every great story has a beginning, a middle and an ending. An effective response to a behavioral-based interview question also has a beginning, a middle and an ending. The content of your response ("your story") must be confident, organized, easy to follow and communicated effectively, so:

- State the specific situation (the beginning)
- Explain the steps to resolution in detail (the middle)
- Share the outcome of the steps you've taken (the ending)

3.   Be mindful of what you say: speak the language of skills. The potential employer will ask questions to determine if you have the

necessary skills for the role and your responses must demonstrate that you do. The only problem is: we don't speak this "language" on a daily basis.

When someone says, "Ericka, how was your day?" I don't reply, "My day was amazing! I effectively communicated information during a 60-minute workshop for 20 attendees. 37% of those in attendance stated their interviewing skills improved thanks to my engaging presentation and my ability to solve problems in the form of questions posed during the session." (Insert pause, blank stare and deep breath.)

My reply contained **skills** and **quantitative data** which is great during an interview but unfortunately, we don't communicate like this on a daily basis.

My suggestion: review the job posting and create a table that aligns your skills with the ones the employer is seeking (see example). Perhaps a mock interview with an experienced professional to ensure your language effectively aligns with the position you seek is a practical next step.

Example

Their candidate requirements:	My qualifications/skills:
Lead a team of 3-5 direct reports	Responsible for 10 direct reports (5 virtual) who manage portfolios and relationships of commercial clients; 5+ years leadership experience

As you prepare for your upcoming interview, incorporate these 3 tips in conjunction with my complimentary interview checklist so you'll be equipped to take your interview to the next level. Lastly, don't ever lose sight of the goal, which is to be prepared and confident so you will ultimately get hired.

To obtain your copy of my interview checklist, please visit www.ErickaSpradley.com .

Article: How To Sell Yourself During The Interview

- "I don't know how to communicate my skills once I'm contacted for an interview."
- "I make it to the interview, but I can't seem to get the job."
- "I want to speak confidently during the interview but interviewing makes me nervous!"

At least one of these challenges will always hold you back from interviewing successfully. The fear, the stress, the nerves, the rejection and the unknown are enough to stop most as they attempt to land a new job. The GREAT news is this doesn't have to be your story. You can overcome your challenges with interviewing to effectively sell yourself when you're equipped with the right information. The secret to selling yourself during an interview is actually what takes place **before** you speak with the employer. You must be willing to work extremely hard to prepare beforehand so you can communicate effectively and with confidence during an interview. If you want to sell yourself during the interview, consider these 3 things as you prepare:

1. What are the responsibilities of the position? Make a list of what the role entails so you can assess how your skills and experiences align with the position.
2. What skills are needed for each responsibility you've listed? For each responsibility you list, identify the skill(s) needed to perform those duties.

3. How should I answer the questions posed? Interviewers want to know if you're the best person for the job. Interviewers want to know if you have the skills to perform once hired. These things are determined based on what you say. With that in mind, capture your BEST examples demonstrating skill proficiency after completing steps 1 and 2. I prepare my responses based on behavioral-based interviews because this format allows me to fully answer the question; providing details, quantitative data and the outcome.

Let's fast forward to the interview; you've evaluated the job posting and are ready for your scheduled appointment. You answer the question "Tell me what you know about this role and the organization" as well as the other background questions. You're now ready to listen attentively to the remaining questions, specifically for the skill within the question. For example, "Tell me about a complex problem you've solved" is the first question. The voice in your head whispers "problem solving", you then answer the question communicating your example of when you've solved a problem. How did you know the employer might ask a question regarding this skill? You aligned the skills needed for the role with the job posting and then organized your thoughtful responses before you arrived. To answer the infamous "how do I sell myself during the interview?" You work extremely hard before you arrive to ensure you're prepared, professional in appearance and are clear about how your skills align with the ones they seek so you can communicate them with confidence.

Additional Support

If you'd like to ensure you're prepared and confident for your next interview, please visit our online store to learn about the following products and services:

- Group Coaching

- 1:1 Coaching

High School Students:

- Career Readiness Camp

- Interview Basics eGuide

Coming Soon:

- Certification Program For Career Center Professionals (High School/College)

- Online courses

Frequently Asked Questions

*How should I use this book? The information is designed to make your approach to interviewing simple. Please don't confuse simple with easy. Interviewing effectively takes time, preparation and practice. I suggest you read each day's information in addition to implementing the activities found in "Your next steps". Feel free to use the margins and spacing in this book to take notes, capture thoughts, etc.

*How much time should I spend preparing for an interview? The amount of time needed for preparation will vary depending on the individual. It depends on the position applied for, your experience with interviewing and your comfort level. I recommend at least 5 hours.

*Should I have someone practice with me? Yes. I suggest you have an experienced professional or someone who interviews successfully review your prepared responses and then provide feedback. Doing so will allow you to present yourself in the best possible light during your interview.

*What interview services do you offer? I offer individual coaching for mock interviews, an extensive coaching program designed to assist individuals regardless of previous interview experience and our downloadable concept, 4-Step Interview Prep. Please visit the online store at www.ErickaSpradley.com for additional information.

*Do you offer resume services? I offer a resume critique for clients who participate in my coaching programs.

About the Author

Ericka Spradley began working at 16, securing her first leadership role in her early 20's.

Interviewing successfully:

- Opened doors to employment (provided financial stability)
- Created self-awareness
- Increased her confidence personally and professionally

Prepared.Confident.Hired! isn't just something to read on Ericka's website, it's actually a lifestyle. She has put in the work; hours of sweat equity full of practice and attention to detail while preparing for interviews. She had (and still does have) the faith to believe in her dreams as well as her skill set which positively impacts confidence and whether or not she's hired. With this in mind, Ericka plans to spend the rest of her life equipping, empowering and encouraging others to successfully secure employment with confidence.

Among her significant accomplishments:

- VP of Professional Development National Society of Collegiate Scholars (NSCS) Strayer University Chapter
- Adjunct Professor College and Career Readiness (Central Piedmont Community College)
- Yahoo! Career Contributor/Columnist
- Career Advisor University of the People
- Ask Ericka (Career Advice Column/Career Contributor)- MetrolinaJobs.com
- Communications Officer and Professional Development Officer for a Women's Network

In addition, her works can be found via The Ladders blog, Today's Charlotte Woman, NSHMBA Magazine, Relevant Magazine and she has also been quoted by The Charlotte Observer as well as Advance Magazine.

Made in the USA
Charleston, SC
31 December 2015